GW00361027

QUAD BIKE STYLE

First Published in Great Britain 2018 by Mirador Publishing

First edition: 2018

Any reference to real names and places are purely fictional and are constructs of the author. Any offence the references produce is unintentional and in no way reflects the reality of any locations or people involved.

A copy of this work is available through the British Library.

ISBN: 978-1-912601-07-3

Mirador Publishing
Mirador
Wearne Lane
Langport
Somerset
TA10 9HB

Quad Bike Style

By

Jan Millward

Also by the author

Tiny Caring Gestures
Gentle Sweet Reminders
Ssh... It Happens! Rural Rhymes from Ryme Intrinseca
Shh... It Happened Again! More Rural Rhymes
Recent Rhyming Rambles

Introduction

I just can't stop myself! This is my sixth book of poetry and I have gone back to my farming roots with another look at life down on the farm.

This book is for all those who appreciate the humour required to work in the great outdoors, especially when animals are involved!

Anyone who has a knowledge of farming and the characters that help shape our landscape will understand!

Quad Bike Style.

Whatever did we use before Quad bikes?

I've heard of plaits and bunches
and a tidy little crop.
Hair woven up and pinned tight
in a bun right on the top.

I know folk who have an Afro',
I've seen mullets and a bob.
I've seen farmers cut their own hair,
and not make a bad job.

I've seen dreadlocks long and matted
and French plaits for the girls.
But the one you see on farmers
is the fresh blown quad bike curl.

They start off fairly normal,
then jump aboard the quad.
Wind blows up in their faces,
and they come back looking odd.

The breeze has done it's magic,
the hair forms a mighty curl.
It rolls around their faces
in a giant backcombed squirl.

They end up looking windswept
when they've been round the flock.
Like they've grabbed hold of some fencing
and they've had a nasty shock.

I don't think this trend will catch on,
The farmers' quad bike style.
But next time when you see one,
it is sure to make you smile!

The Shepherd.

This poem is dedicated to all the hard working shepherds out there.
The real life Bo Peeps!

The north wind is blowing and it's blooming freezing,
the snowflakes are falling, there's no sign it's easing.
It's minus a lot and there's sheep to be fed,
and all that I want is my nice cosy bed.

I poke out my nose and feel the cold air.
I reach for my clothes in a heap on the chair.
I grab my thick socks and go under the sheets,
whilst trying to hold on to the last of the heat.

Layers upon layers of jumpers and shirts,
and trousers with yesterday's dried on old dirt.
A quick wipe with a flannel and brush of the teeth,
and not too much care of what lies underneath.

The moon is now shining on fresh fallen snow,
I'm now in my coat and my face is aglow.
I pull on my hat and my gloves with the liners,
you've never seen a woman look any finer!

All that's on view is a pair of blue eyes,
I look like a Womble in a woolly disguise.
My fingers are starting to freeze on the tips,
I breathe out frosted air from weather chapped lips.

I slip on the ice and fall down like a pin.
I never get hurt 'cause I'm padded not thin.
I curse and I mutter and brush off the snow,
ignoring the chilblains that itch on my toe.

And when I am happy that everything's fed,
and settled and comfy with straw for a bed.
I go back to the house for a hot cup of tea,
but have to strip off so I can have a wee.

The coats are all dripping and starting to steam,
The life of a shepherd just living the dream.
A lamb by the fire, a dog by the door
and a wind screaming wildly around the top moor.

Farm Girls.

There is nothing quite as versatile as a farm girl. Criticise at your own risk!

You may criticise our make-up,
you can laugh about our teeth.
You can think we have no feelings,
but don't know what lies beneath.

You can laugh at all the farm girls
with broken fingernails,
the ones in dirty overalls
and muck from off cows' tails.

You may scoff at farmer tan lines,
the straw stuck in our hair.
But please don't try and judge us
that really isn't fair.

You may think it really funny
that we get straw in our bras,
but we will get our own back
when you're following in your car.

Because farm girls can drive tractors
and we will go so slow,
if you drive too close behind us
and we have no place to go.

And please don't patronise us,
we know how to castrate.
It's much better to respect us,
then we can be great mates.

Don't snipe about our cattle
or snigger at our sheep,
we have the skills if needed
that could make a grown man weep.

Farm girls they are the toughest,
they know all their stock by name.
They can deal with cows at calving
and sort out sheep when lame.

They can service the old tractor
and bale up fields of hay.
Stay up all night lambing
and mend the fence by day.

They can spot a sickly heifer,
milk a herd of cattle.
Ride a stroppy pony
as if they're going to battle.

They can plough the fields and scatter,
the good seed on the land.
Train a bull to halter
and be there to lend a hand.

And sometimes they achieve this
with a kid or two in tow,
and still have hair that's shiny
and cheeks that are all aglow.

Don't underestimate a farm girl,
many are college trained.
There is a lot more to it
than cooking on the range.

But when you get to know them
you will find a heart of gold,
and if you find a good one
you will live to be quite old!

One In Every Village.

There has certainly been one of these characters in every village I have lived in.
Is there one in yours?

There's one in every village,
you will see her curtains twitch.
The one, two hundred years ago
would be branded as a witch.

She's the one who knows your business
before you do yourself.
And it's best to just ignore her
if you value your good health.

If someone has a baby,
or they're having an affair.
You'll see her in the window,
watching from her chair.

And she'll spread around the gossip
like confetti at a wedding.
She'll even tell the neighbours
when you change your bedding.

She makes everything her business,
she'll know the colour of your knickers.
She'll be waiting in the churchyard
to see who's chatting to the vicar.

And if you have just moved in
she'll invite herself to tea,
to check the colour of your curtains
and find out your history.

We don't worry about break-ins,
she's like a private guard.
She'd be asking them for details
before they crossed the yard.

And she'll check on poor old Ethel
and bore her half to death,
about the price of milk and taters
and hardly draw a breath.

There's one in every village,
it's as if they share them out.
From a school for nosey neighbours,
sprinkled carefully about.

And when she finally goes to
that heavenly village in the sky,
you know she'll still be watching
like a celestial village spy!

Farm Kids.

Children lucky enough to grow up on farms are a special breed indeed!

There are kids that grow up normal
and drink milk out of a bottle.
And then there are the farm kids
who have lives lived at full throttle.

To farm kids it is normal
to spend days out in the sun.
Climbing trees and getting muddy
is their idea of fun.

Helping to move cattle,
standing in a gap.
Knowing the small difference
between a mushroom and Death Cap.

Feeding lambs by bottle,
holding the torch for Dad.
Helping with a calving,
the happy times and sad.

Knowing the importance
of shutting all the gates.
Talking to the chickens
with a dog that's your best mate.

A little pair of overalls,
spending life in wellies.
Helping in the parlour,
not caring if you're smelly.

Knowing names of flowers,
picking out the weeds.
Pulling up the thistles
before they make the seeds.

Taking out the sandwiches
and sitting in the fields.
Listening to the cowman
talking about the yields.

Knowing what needs doing,
learning common sense.
Handing out the staples
when Dad's mending an old fence.

Learning to drive a tractor
before you're even ten.
You'll know when you are ready,
no one can tell you when.

Riding a small pony
over little home-made jumps.
Not caring about bruises
scratches, lumps and bumps.

Sliding down snowy hillsides
on bags stuffed full of straw,
making dens in treetops
who could want for more?

Going home exhausted
with a smile upon your face.
Pockets full of conkers,
a life no one could replace!

Church.

This was a big part of my childhood. Church was the place to meet up with our friends and scare the living daylights out of each other playing hide and seek in the churchyard after choir practice!

All those years of going to church
with bottoms numb on wooden perch.
The Sunday morning boring preach,
whilst we dreamt of fun down at the beach.

The vicar dressed in white attire,
trying to light our inner fire.
Miss Harper always at full throttle
and George the warden on the bottle.

And us as girls put in the choir,
in cassocks that we thought were dire.
We swung on the ropes for the bell
and Miss Roberts said we'd go to hell.

The hymns we murdered by the line,
although we liked "Shine, Jesus shine".
Miss Frampton in her flowery frock,
the ticking of the vestry clock.

The ladies who did altar flowers,
they stayed behind for hours and hours.
Collection plates for our donations,
prayers for all the third world nations.

Old farmer Jones would go to sleep,
worn out from chasing wayward sheep.
His wife would poke him in despair,
but he just snored, he didn't care.

The promise of eternal life,
the wedding vows twixt man and wife.
The funerals and the sad goodbyes,
the heaven promised in the skies.

Collections for the old church roof,
agnostics looking for more proof.
The crack of knees knelt on the floor,
the draught that crept in through the door.

At harvest time, big sheaves of wheat,
with thank you's for the food we eat.
The loaves of bread, the bowls of fruit,
farm workers stuffed in shiny suits.

At Christmas out would come the stable,
a change from all that Cain and Abel.
With candles glowing in the night,
giving out a gentle light.

At midnight mass the drunks came in
to try and save themselves from sin.
And then it was all "Deck the Halls"
with spindly trees covered in balls.

At Easter we wanted lots of treats.
We smuggled chocolate in our seats.
We warbled "Christ is risen today,"
and nibbled eggs when we could pray.

For Mothers' Day we got some flowers,
the service seemed to last for hours.
We raced to give them to our mother,
trying to beat our little brother.

And as we heard the church bell chime,
we were learning all the time.
We learned respect and the Lord's prayer
and we were taught it's good to share.

And we made friends and had a laugh,
as regular as our weekly bath.
In Sunday best with our collection,
days remembered with great affection.

And when we go to church today,
our knees now creak when we must pray.
We sing the hymns, praise to our God
and try and tread where saints have trod.

Please Be Safe.

Farming by its very nature can be a dangerous profession;
it's up to each of us to work safely.

Please be safe down on the farm,
we don't want you to come to harm.
Please take heed, it's not too late
to take control of your own fate.

When you are out and all alone,
always take your mobile phone.
It might just be your only link,
just take a moment, stop and think.

Old tractors should have a roll bar
even if you don't go that far.
Somebody else might have a go
and they can tip, however slow.

Make sure your guards are all in place,
however busy, do not race.
You don't want on your epitaph
"He didn't want to wait for staff".

Respect your stock, and never ever
try to outwit them, that's not clever.
However many years you've farmed
there is a chance that you'll be harmed.

A farmer is against the clock,
baling hay and checking stock.
We all take risks, but take the time
to think it through and you'll be fine.

And if you have lagoons of slurry
make sure they're fenced, it is a worry.
Kids love to play around the yard
but check your fences, it's not that hard.

Enjoy the life, it is the best,
you work long hours, have little rest.
A moments thought will save you pain
and keeps you safe to farm again.

Happy.

Home is certainly where the heart is.

Happy are the moments spent behind closed doors
with no one to criticise or point out all your flaws.
Hang up your coat and dump your bag upon a chair,
and feel all the tension melt away into the air.

Fill up the kettle, lock the world out of your space.
Let down your guard and feel a smile spread on your face.
Batten down the hatch and leave your cares behind,
it's in your own sanctuary that you'll find peace of mind.

Forget the little trials that wear your spirit down,
leave on the step those thoughts that make you frown.
Relax and let go of the stresses of the day,
shut out the negativity and throw your cares away.

Home is the place where you can be yourself.
Curl up by the fire, take your book down off the shelf.
It's a precious safe haven in a world lived at full pace
so take your foot off the pedal and forget about the race.

Good Luck Lambers!

It is so easy to gaze at cute lambs skipping in fields and not be aware of the hard work that has gone on behind that idyllic scene.

Good luck to all you lambers
I hope you get some sleep.
If you have too much trouble,
you could try counting sheep!

A shout to all the ladies,
with broken fingernails,
carrying buckets of ewe nuts,
in paper sacks and pails.

Good luck to all you shepherds
with weary arms and legs.
Out with gel and torches,
checking on the tegs.

I'm thinking of you farmers
leaving your cosy beds,
with PJ's tucked in wellies
inspecting ewes in sheds.

Three cheers to all the workers
with purple stains and scratches.
Heads bent against the weather,
battening down the hatches.

To those of you who smell like
you haven't washed for days.
Who don't know what the time is
and nights pass in a haze.

Well done to those young students
who are willing to work hard,
keeping everything going
and tidying up the yard.

To all who have bruised fingers,
with straw stuck in their hair.
Who deal with all the problems
when life seems far from fair.

To those who are eating muesli
because they haven't time to shop.
Having to keep on going,
working until they drop.

Well done to all our shepherds
you really are the best.
And when lambing is all over
make sure you get a rest!

Ratio: High And Low.

How times have changed!

When I learned to drive a tractor
oh so many years ago,
it had no bells and whistles,
it did stop and pretty slow.

The brakes were independent,
if you removed the catch.
Then you could corner nicely
as you rode around the patch.

The seat had a small cushion
made from a hessian sack,
padded out with lumpy cotton,
and it nearly broke your back.

There was no power steering
and if you hit a rock,
it would nearly break your fingers
and you'd get a nasty shock.

If you were very lucky
you might have had a cab,
with mucky plastic windows
that were ripped and pretty drab.

It was always very noisy,
so earmuffs were a must.
If you were rowing hay up
you'd need a mask against the dust.

If you were spreading bag muck
you lined up with the hedge.
There were no flashy satellites,
this was farming on the edge.

To stop the three point linkage
swaying wildly to and fro,
you tied it all together
and maintained a status quo.

And when the day was over
you would park up in the yard,
with a can on the exhaust pipe
if it was raining hard.

If you had trouble steering
and the front was up in the air
the cowman could sit on the bonnet,
you knew he wouldn't care.

You didn't have a radio,
there was no mobile phone.
If you found you had a breakdown,
you were usually on your own.

Tractors are now so massive
compared to what I know.
But give me a little tractor
with a ratio high and low.

Goats.

I ain't afraid of no goats!

You may have pigs and chickens
but the ones who really gloat,
say you don't know what real love is
until you've owned a goat.

The goatie folk are special,
they will like a certain breed.
Anglo-Nubian or Saanen,
they'll pamper their every need.

You might find it quite frustrating
when they get out in your plants.
They will even eat your washing,
your T shirts and your pants.

But don't upset your goat herd
or complain that goats are smelly,
even if the grumpy Billy
has chewed holes in your best wellies.

You'll be told that goats are special
and you'll never understand,
that their itsy bitsy hoof prints
will help improve your land.

But once you get addicted
it will never stop at two,
soon goats will be appearing
in every place you view.

And don't attempt to fence them
the same as you would sheep.
They'll destroy a six foot hurdle,
they can make a grown man weep.

Goats aren't good at grazing,
they much prefer to browse.
They are partial to most hedgerows,
your jacket and your blouse.

And if you have to milk them
keep a hold on that full bucket,
they'll do their best to kick it
and you might just say **** it.

I see them in the summer
when we go around the shows,
standing on the hurdles
trying to grab your clothes.

I love to see the goats out,
those stubborn Roman noses.
Peeking around the borders
whilst eating all the roses.

But goats are really friendly
and you might catch the bug
but if they get too naughty,
point out you need a rug!

Tribute to the Land Girls.

This poem is a tribute to my mum and also my lovely Aunty May.

In the dark days of the forties,
when Britain was at war,
the men all got their call up,
and had to leave these shores.

The country stood united,
they had to fight the foe.
The women took their places
as they watched their menfolk go.

And some went in the factories
and helped to make the bombs.
All stood up to be counted,
the daughters and their mums.

But thousands from the cities
went to work the land.
They knew that they were needed,
they had to make a stand.

They joined the Women's Land Army,
the WLA.
They soon were in the country,
milking cows and making hay.

They supported the old farmers
who didn't go to war.
They grew the nation's rations,
they filled the country's stores.

And it was never ever easy,
the work was hard and long.
They took up to the challenge,
together they were strong.

They saw the planes fly over,
they watched their cities burn.
They fought their war with pitchforks,
they knew it was their turn.

Hairdressers and shop girls
in dungarees and boots.
Digging up the pastures,
picking beans and fruits.

Farming for our future,
learning on the spot.
Missing all their families,
but giving their best shot.

They wore the badge of freedom
as they worked upon the land,
something our generation
will never understand.

A nation of strong women
who stood above the clouds of war.
We must vow that we'll remember
what they were fighting for.

The Land Girls Of Today.

And this is a tribute to the land girls of today!

String in all your pockets,

straw stuck in your bra.

Syringes in the kitchen,

feed bags in the car.

Penknife in your pocket,

ear tags in the hall.

Wellies lined up waiting,

leggings by the wall.

Stacks of Farmers Weekly's

piled up in the loo.

Overalls for soaking,

caked in dried on poo.

Trails of wheat and barley,

little bits of hay.

Clues to what is happening,

on the farm today.

Pessaries in handbags,

picked up from the vets.

AI man on speed dial,

so you don't forget.

Looks from other parents
when you turn up on a tractor,
and they are clean and tidy
with make-up by Max Factor.
Coats that smell of silage,
a hat controls your hair.
Carrots in your pocket
to bribe a stroppy mare.
Quad bike and a trailer,
windblown cheeks aglow.
Grubby hands and fingers,
a chilblain on your toe.
Not everybody gets it,
it's hard to understand.
But those who do won't change it,
a life worked on the land.

Knickers.

Here's a gentle rummage through your drawers!

We all have a drawer of knickers
that range from sexy to drab.
The ones we wear everyday are
the first ones that we grab.

They are our big girls' knickers,
with comfort guaranteed.
When we are out there working,
these are the ones we need.

We all have packs of new ones
waiting patiently in reserve.
And the ones when we feel skinny
and ones to fit every curve.

We all have a few best ones
edged round in fancy lace.
Red and black and racy,
sexy is no disgrace.

And what about the old ones,
for when you're feeling flabby?
The ones with little roses
that now look rather shabby.

And then the nice and normal
for when you see the nurse.
With a spare pair in a handbag
inside a big old purse.

The six pairs for your holiday,
you select those for their youth.
In case you get stopped at the airport,
(you don't want to seem uncouth).

The ones you pick out monthly,
for when you are feeling a grump.
They hold you all together
when you're looking for someone to thump.

And then the ones you purchased,
whilst feeling quite spontaneous.
That fit more like a cheese string
and feel almost subcutaneous.

And if you go out shopping
and end up in a changing room,
you hope you've put on some good ones
to show off your va va voom!

But if you are a farmer
some may be stained purple or blue.
If you messed up with the spray can,
the colour goes right through!

Home Early.

This is my husband.
Being a Welshman he always says that he will be there now in a minute!

I'll be home tonight quite early,
I promise I won't be late.
I've got to roll the paddock,
then mend Six Acres gate.

I know that it's your birthday
and you've booked the local pub.
I'll make sure that I'm finished,
I like their lovely grub.

I am aiming for six thirty
if everything goes to plan,
but I've got to pick up wormer
and there's no diesel in the van.

Yes I know you don't go out much,
that's the trouble with a farm.
But I need to check the heifers
and bed down in the old barn.

I forgot to let the rams out,
it won't take very long.
I'm sure they will be waiting,
but I'll hurry them along.

Yes I know that you are ready,
but I've just met poor old Bill.
I couldn't just walk past him,
'cause his wife's been rather ill.

I just have to change the battery
on the top field electric fence,
I'm really trying to hurry
and you're sounding rather tense.

There's an oil leak on the tractor
I've tried to patch it up,
then I tried to take a short cut
I was knocked down by a tup.

But don't worry I'm not bleeding,
I just have some mild concussion.
But I will be with you in a minute
there's no need to get a fuss on.

I know we're meeting Peter
and his perfect wife called Gill,
but I'm covered in oil and cow muck
and I'm feeling slightly ill.

I know they will look perfect,
but I'll bleach off all the stains,
and I need to cover the silage
because Bill says it might rain.

Look I'm sorry, but please stop ringing,
I will be about half an hour.
Could you make me a quick sandwich?
I can eat it in the shower.

If you look behind the wellies
you'll find I left your present.
There is no need to thank me,
I know you love a pheasant.

And I'll try to stay awake when
Pete moans about his day.
Sat at his work computer
while we were hauling hay.

Oh and while I order diesel
could you iron my favourite shirt?
It's the one behind the drier
(please check for specks of dirt).

Thanks for being patient,
I know you understand.
It's not easy loving a farmer
when they're married to their land.

Morris Minor.

What was your first car?
The ones I used to drive are now only seen at vintage rallies!

I miss the cars of yesteryear,
the ones that only had four gears.
The gentle pulling of the choke,
the slate grey clouds of oily smoke.

I miss the blanket on my knee,
back then air con' you got for free.
The flooding of the carburettor,
pumping the throttle made it wetter.

The feeler gauge for setting points,
the greasing up of rusty joints.
Spraying the distributor cap,
breaking down and having a nap.

Waiting for the RAC
with pickled egg and cup of tea.
No mobile phone to summon aid,
you'd start to walk but wish you'd stayed.

Pumping the brakes after a flood,
Push-start and falling in the mud.
The boiling of the radiator,
kicking the wheel and saying you hate her.

Headlights that filled up in the rain,
the flutter valve, that fine membrane.
The fan belt mended with a stocking,
the engine that was always knocking.

An aerial on the front bonnet,
car tax with the date stuck on it.
The dipstick always reading low,
you had two speeds then, stop and go.

The worry when the light came on,
you didn't know where the oil had gone.
Temperature gauges on the red,
brakes back then had to be bled.

The hope when you tried a cold start,
that dying noise could break your heart.
Moss that grew on window frames
that has all gone, oh what a shame!

I miss my little Morris Minor,
in Racing Green, there was none finer.
But now I can get from A to B,
without a blanket on my knee!

Dad.

The old characters are what make farming so special.

If my old dad could see us now,
he'd have a look at every cow.
He'd lean across the old field gate,
just like he did each day at eight.

He'd see the stock through wise old eyes,
he knew the weather from the skies.
Old wisdom stored inside his head.
A farmer born, a farmer bred.

He knew the land, the fields, the brook.
He'd put us straight with just a look.
He'd work so far into the night,
he made sure everything was right.

He ploughed a furrow straight and true.
No GPS then, he just knew.
He had the way of folk back then,
the strong and wise old countrymen.

I see him now with stick in hand,
a man who truly knew the land.
The world has changed, the shadows fall
his cap still hangs in our old hall.

What would he think of all the hate
that people bring to the farm gate?
The ones who think that we do wrong,
I know he'd want us to be strong.

So stand up tall and fill those boots
we are the ones at the grass roots.
Lead by example, work the land
and try and help folk understand.

Man Ban.

The world has gone quite mad!

It seems there now is a strange ban,
which stops us using the word "man".
A manhole covers name is banned,
across all of this pleasant land.

We now must say it is for "persons".
I really can't think of a worse one.
A "person hole" is far from nice,
it strikes of things loaded with vice.

That common phrase "man on the street"
we've always used, it's rather neat.
But "person" rears its ugly head,
and "average person" must be said.

If someone is asked to man the desk,
be careful it may be a test.
Now it is only done by "staff".
I think someone must like a laugh.

And nothing now is made by man.
It seems it's part of this sad ban.
We now must say it's artificial.
It all seems just so superficial.

We do not say waitress and waiters,
it had to come sooner or later.
Now they are simply called a server,
(this is bound to cause a fervour).

And never call a fireman out.
Firefighters is the word about.
Please try not to be workman like,
or everyone will go on strike.

A chairman used to be the one,
to lead the team, now that is gone.
Now you must only please say chair,
to try and make life very fair.

Sportsmanship is also dead,
we must all say fairness instead.
It isn't easy to be right,
in this grey world, no black or white.

The housewife now is also gone.
I think this is just one big con.
She now is called just a consumer,
if you believe all of the rumours.

We can't now say our Christian name,
in case we try and hand out blame.
Our forefathers would not be pleased
to know that name has now been seized.

The thought police think they are kind,
but they are messing with my mind.
I like a man who opens doors,
they want to fill the world with bores.

I think it has gone far enough,
the world is hard and very tough.
Don't label us as all the same,
we sometimes need a man to blame!

Silage.

Do you remember your own husband
now that silage has begun?
If you're lucky you might see him
grab a sandwich on the run.
The weather's fair and settled
and we're feeling like we're jilted,
'cause the tractor wheels are turning
now that the grass is wilted.

Ready To Go.

When it's ready, it's ready!

They have greased up the old mower,
and lined the silage pit.
They have watched the weather forecast
and everything is fit.

The trailers have their sides on,
the buck rake's on the tractor.
The guys have dug their flasks out,
and they've phoned up the contractors.

Everybody's ready,
the sun is shining bright,
and sandwiches and KitKats
will keep them going through the night.

The grass is cut and wilting,
the sugar's running high.
The forager starts grunting
under a clear blue sky.

The tractors and the trailers
are driving to and fro.
The cowman moves his cattle,
and then goes off to mow.

The forager is roaring
like an angry beast.
Eating up the acres
for a winter feast.

The driver of the buck rake
is building a neat heap,
rolling all the air out,
reversing, beep beep beep.

It needs some concentration
to roll right to the edge,
with one wheel in the silage
and the other on a ledge.

The sweat drips off the drivers
and the empty trailers rattle,
and the smell of sun and silage
attracts the neighbour's cattle.

The sun is getting lower
and the sky has turned blood red,
but they will keep on going
as others go to bed.

With one eye on the weather,
they will try and fill the clamp,
until the dew starts forming
and the grass is getting damp.

Then they will park up ready
to do it all again,
and pray the sun keeps shining
and drives away the rain.

And when they take their boots off
their socks are full of bits,
which they walk up to the bathroom,
before they take off all their kit.

There's grass inside the toilet
and stuck around the shower,
is dirt and dust and grass seeds
and a daisy in full flower.

Good luck to all on silage,
it's long hard hours each day,
but just be blooming grateful
it's not small bales of hay!

The Old Farmer.

Farming for the next generation.

He never takes his cap off,
it seems welded to his head.
The cowman reckons he wears it
even when he goes to bed.

He wears the same old jacket
in snow and summer's sun.
His pockets are full of cough sweets
and a cartridge for his gun.

He wears faded moleskin trousers
with string around the waist.
He keeps a penknife and some matches
and a pound note just in case.

And his ancient moss green jumper
that's been darned up by his wife,
is the one he got at market
and he's kept it all his life.

His boots are worn and covered
in dubbin from a tin.
They've seen him through some tough times,
but now are wearing thin.

He can't stop a pig in a passage,
his legs are locked and bowed.
His back is bent by his farming
and all the fields he's ploughed.

His eyes are full of wisdom,
he has seen a lot of change.
He's never left the village
and some new folk think he's strange.

His hands are gnarled and curled up,
his face is lined and red.
He still likes to have a potter
with his old tools in his shed.

But behind the worn out body
is a man who loves the land,
who knows each tree and hedgerow,
though not everyone understands.

His instinct for his livestock
he didn't get from a book.
It's from years of observation
whilst leaning on his crook.

He's from a generation
that understood the need
to farm for the next generation
and for that we should pay heed.

Pine Fresh Green.

There's nowt wrong with a bit of dirt, as long as it's clean dirt!

Our house was very different
when I was just a child.
Coal fire was our heating,
when winter winds were wild.

The windows always rattled
against the winter's storm.
Our back was always freezing,
our front was always warm.

There was no central heating,
ice formed on window panes.
We sometimes used a bucket,
if the roof leaked in the rain.

Hot water bottles stopped us
freezing in our beds.
No tog filled cosy duvets,
we had eiderdowns instead.

We didn't have a bathroom,
the toilet was outside.
If it was dark and windy
a torch would be our guide.

Remember scratchy paper
and a carton full of Vim?
And the door was propped half open
if the light was growing dim.

We washed with jugs of water,
and bathed just once a week.
Washed our hair in smelly Vosene
until it nearly squeaked.

Mum was always cooking,
we ate big pots of stew.
There were dumplings in the gravy
that stuck to ribs like glue.

We didn't have to worry
about the sell by date.
We sniffed and checked for insects
and left the rest to fate!

We climbed up trees and paddled
in muddy brooks and streams.
We rolled down banks and hillsides
in the childhood of my dreams.

Our clothes were patched and ragged
and passed right down the line.
We did not have much money,
but we all turned out fine.

The times they are a changing,
the world keeps moving on.
We wash and clean and scrub up,
until all the germs are gone.

Now we're always sparkling
and everything is clean.
The toilet has a freshener,
and the water's pine fresh green.

But something now is missing,
cleaning has gone too far.
And we have to drink bacteria,
in a handy little jar!

Relationship Rules For Men.

Pay attention, gentlemen. These are tried and tested rules!

If you are newly married
there are some things you need to know.
If you want your love to blossom,
this is how your love will grow.

Never ever tell her
that's she's put on a bit of weight,
or say that she's more curvy
than on that sweet first date.

Don't tell her she looks puffy,
or mention bloodshot eyes.
She never will forget it,
and she'll use it to chastise.

Don't criticise her cooking,
or say your mum knows best.
She will set out to entrap you,
she'll see it as a test.

Don't ogle other women
when you're walking up the street,
or say that they look gorgeous
or you like them quite petite.

And if she ever tells you
she has nothing left to wear,
don't open up her wardrobe
even for a dare.

Don't even try a cuddle
if she is feeling down,
and back off several inches
if she starts to frown.

And never ever call her
by your exe's name,
or she will try to maim you,
she will have a perfect aim.

Don't buy her clothes for Christmas
if you get them way too small.
Or you will find your suitcase
packed and waiting in the hall.

You will learn the hard way
that you never must forget,
birthdays and anniversaries
and the place that you first met.

And if she's feeling poorly
or has had a trying day,
don't ask her where your tea is
if you want your love to say.

If she is somewhat moody
don't ask if it's the week,
when she gets tired and cranky
or your future may be bleak.

And if you say you'll be home
by a certain time,
you must try your best to make it,
late is another crime.

Don't criticise her driving,
just keep looking straight ahead.
A bitten tongue is better,
some things are best unsaid.

Don't put her pic' on Facebook
unless she has passed it first,
that is a great big no no
and you'll be forever cursed.

If she keeps sheep and cattle
she won't tell you to your face.
But they will be her favourites,
you will have to learn your place.

But if she really loves you
she won't ever want another,
as long as you don't ever
say she's turned into her mother!

The Bridesmaid.

Don't worry, no one is perfect!

I've been asked to be a bridesmaid
to a very good friend of mine.
She's petite and she's gorgeous
and I know she'll look divine.

I know I'll have to do it,
I would never let her down,
but the others will look perfect
in strapless turquoise gowns.

The rest work in an office,
they work out daily in a gym.
They drink milkshakes for their dinner
and always look so slim.

But I work as a farmer
and my back is broad and wide.
If I had to walk beside her
there'd be no room for the bride.

I have muscles on my muscles,
and in a dress that has no sleeves.
I won't look much like a Stephanie
but more like a guy called Steve.

I have bruises on my shoulders
from where I fell off the barn roof,
and to top off this wondrous image
I have also cracked a tooth.

My feet are used to wellies,
I fear I might break an ankle,
but I found some flattish slip-ons,
so at least for that I'm thankful.

Those girls are really lovely
with perfect painted nails,
but if you milk cows for a living
your hands are bound to fail.

The day is fast approaching
and I'm feeling like a mess,
but I go out for a try on
of my turquoise bridesmaid's dress.

But then I feel much happier,
we're getting a little cape.
It wraps around my shoulders
and hides my farmer shape.

And the others try and help me,
they shape and preen and pluck.
I wedge my feet into my sandals,
but I'm walking like a duck.

On the day the bride looks glorious,
and I put my fears aside.
I do my best to try and walk straight
and not to waddle, but to glide.

And then I see my husband,
he is glowing with pure pride,
and as I walk on past him
he can see how hard I've tried.

So girls it may not matter
if we're not perfect every day.
Because if you chose the right man
he'll love you anyway!

Living The Dream.

We don't all lean on gates sucking straw!

There's a hole in my welly
and I'm feeling damp.
The muck's seeping in
and my toes have got cramp.

I smell of stale milk
and wet brewer's grains,
my jeans have a rip
and there's stains on my stains.

I dropped my new phone
when I scraped up the slurry,
I plunged in my hand
because I had to hurry.

And stuck up my sleeve
going green on my arm,
some of the stuff
that you find on a farm.

There's poo in my hair
and it's dried on all crusty.
I find my old coat
and it smells stale and musty.

I slip in the yard
on thirteen's placenta,
and my jeans turned a shade
of deep red magenta.

My glasses are speckled
I'm struggling to see,
and all that I want
is a hot cup of tea.

My clothes are now damp
and I'm starting to steam,
and most wouldn't see
that I'm living the dream.

Life on the farm
is not like on the telly,
they don't show the muck
and you can't tell it's smelly.

They all wear clean clothes
and red checked plaid shirts,
and wellies that never
get to see any dirt.

They don't show the times
when the sheep have got out,
or mention the language
and the things that we shout.

And everyone thinks
that we're all a bit slow,
and think that it's all
like they see on the show.

But we are the ones
who put food on your plate,
even when we look rough
and our clothes are a state.

And that's how it is
when you work on the land,
take a new look
and you might understand.

Grumpy.

We all get those days when the world seems to be against us.

When you are down and feeling grumpy,
when someone's called you short and stumpy.
When everyone is on your back
and you have taken too much flak.

Just walk away and clear your mind,
don't let it in and you will find,
it doesn't matter what they say
and you will cope in your own way.

Remember life is far too short,
just like a flower we need support.
Walk away from those who hate,
good things will come to those who wait.

The ones who talk behind your back,
and sneak about in a small pack,
must have a life that's very sad,
to want your life to turn out bad.

So smile and lift your chin up high,
ignore the ones who like to pry.
Surround yourself with those who care,
and you will find you've love to spare!

Relief.

We all are only human. (Even mother's-in-law)!

I cleaned the house from top to bottom,
not one small corner was forgotten.
I wiped the skirtings, cleaned the sills,
filled vases full of daffodils.

I scrubbed the sink and bleached the loo,
did everything I had to do.
I sprayed all rooms with " Lotus bean",
the brass pot glowed, the windows gleamed.

The wet and dry sucked up the dirt,
the flower pots had a watery squirt.
I even cleaned the cupboards out,
and threw away some mouldy sprouts.

The scene was set, the cushions plumped,
the green potatoes chucked and dumped.
The coffee tables set with mats,
the hallway stripped of all it's tat.

The wellies banished to the shed,
and gleaming tiles shone out instead.
No sign of straw walked through the hall,
nothing to criticise at all.

The dog was groomed and had clean paws
and dirt was wiped off all the doors.
I thought I'd done a thorough job,
to prove I wasn't just a slob.

Then she arrived, new mum-in-law,
she looked amazed at the clean floor.
I put the kettle on for tea,
chose unchipped mugs for her and me.

And then my kids came running in,
covered in mud, making a din.
They slid across the sparkling floor
and wiped some cow muck on the door.

I nearly cried but she said to me,
"The best things in life are always free.
Life is too short so please don't worry.
You're lucky he's not spreading slurry".

"It's nice to have the time to clean,
but please don't treat me like a queen.
I once was you and thought the same,
but I will never hand out blame.

"A house must always be a home.
I promise I will never moan.
As long as there is love and joy,
you will be perfect for my boy".

The Lesson.

He'd come to mend the tractor,
he parked up in the yard.
Expecting an old farmer,
the girl caught him off his guard.

She took him through the cowshed
and led him round the back,
the hay was smelling sweetly
rowed up in a neat stack.

She told him that the farmer
was running a bit late.
He said he'd eat his dinner,
he didn't mind a wait.

She told him that she loved him,
she said that she'd be true,
whilst he munched upon a pasty
and poured himself a brew.

She was the cowman's daughter,
so young and very fit,
with hair just like an angel
and clothes covered in sh*t.

He saw her sat there gazing,
he looked into her blue eyes.
He'd come to mend the hydraulics
and his top link started to rise.

But she was looking past him
at a tiny new bull calf,
she caught his look of passion
and broke out into a laugh.

"Oh no!" she told him bluntly.
"These calves they are my life.
If you want love and passion,
look elsewhere for a wife".

He choked upon his pasty,
he apologised and ran,
and blushing very brightly,
rushed back to his work's van.

And then he saw her mother
built like a Hereford bull,
he gabbled that he was going
his words tangled up like wool.

His legs had turned to jelly,
he could barely shut the door.
He made a break for freedom
and put his foot down to the floor.

This lad had learned a lesson,
to respect the young farm lasses.
Because if you step out of kilter
their mums will whip your asses!

Aotearoa.

So many of us nowadays have been lucky enough to have lived and worked in
New Zealand.

Aotearoa, the land of the long white cloud.
A country full of beauty that makes so many proud.
A land steeped in tradition and built by men of passion,
where rugby is a religion and Swannys' are high fashion.

And if you ask a question, it always ends in "Ay".
"Kia Ora" is their greeting, or you might just get "gudday".
And then there are the farmers as tough as seasoned leather,
mustering their flocks regardless of the weather.

If you have read the books by the legend that was Murray,
you'll know a bit about them so you will have no worries.
For Wal he is the image of men up and down that land
with dogs around their ankles and Cooch at their right hand.

The Kiwi's are plain speaking and will always tell it straight,
and love to tell their stories from the farm side of the gate.
They love a sausage sizzle washed down with a few tinnies.
And you will have to step up, this is no place for ninnies.

And you will find the Kiwis are the nicest folk you'll meet,
they don't much like their veggies, but boy they love their meat.
They love to take the micky, especially if you're a Pom,
so just be very careful when you tell them where you're from!

The Annual Flower Show.

This actually happened! Oh the drama!

There's trouble in the village at the annual flower show.
We've admired the rows of veggie's, set out in a neat row.
The cakes and jams look scrummy and good enough to eat,
but Bill has been disqualified and he won't admit defeat.

He had entered in the category "six home grown shallots".
And he'd polished up his entries and tied the stalks in knots.
But in his rush to enter, because he was running late,
he didn't do a count and had put seven on the plate.

After all the judging, which was done behind closed doors,
the prizes were decided and they'd totted up the scores.
Everyone came flocking to see what they had won,
and all were smiling happily, apart from just the one.

Bill couldn't quite believe it when he saw that he'd come last,
he stood alone in silence feeling quite aghast.
His shallots were just amazing, perfect in every way.
But he had put too many and now he had to pay.

He saw old George there gloating, he had won first prize.
He was showing them to Barbara with a twinkle in his eyes.
Bill wasn't in the mood for that, he knew it was just a tease,
but then he suddenly spotted, he'd come first in garden peas!

George.

I think we all know a George.

I love the thrill of market,
the noises and the smell,
the people and the cattle,
the sound of the calling bell.

Old George would always be there,
in greasy ancient cap,
with trousers and crossed braces
and legs set at a gap.

Taking in the glory
of cattle at their peak,
or waiting there on Thursday
when folk come to sell their sheep.

Leaning on his stick
with a twinkle in his eye.
Checking all the livestock,
but he doesn't come to buy.

This has been his journey,
farming all his life.
Growing old and lonely
after he lost his wife.

The market is his lifeline,
it's full of his old friends.
He notes down all the prices,
he follows all the trends.

And no one walks right past him
without a friendly chat,
a moan about the weather
tales of this and that.

He buys a bacon butty
and his favourite steaming brew,
and settles by the ringside
where he gets a better view.

He chats with all the drivers,
the stockmen and the hands,
the farmers and the youngsters
who now work on the land.

He's been part of this old market
since he was just a boy.
He's loved by everybody
and it fills his heart with joy.

And when George hangs up his jacket
and leaves behind this life,
we hope he'll be reunited
with Molly his dear wife.

And the market will fall silent,
they'll remember their old friend.
A gentleman and farmer
right to the very end.

Eau De Welly.

Happy memories!

It's Saturday, the fire is lit.
It's my turn to sit down a bit.
I've had a soak in a Radox bath,
and I'm watching tele' for a laugh.

PJ's are on and dressing gown.
I've washed off all that's green and brown.
A bag of crisps, a glass of wine,
my evening is looking just fine.

The dog is curled up on the floor,
relaxed and letting out a snore.
The lights are dimmed, the curtains drawn.
I stretch my legs and have a yawn.

And just as my eyes start to close
and I settle for a cosy doze,
I hear the phone ring pierce the air,
I leap up from my comfy chair.

My neighbour says the cows are out,
I say there is no need to shout.
I ask her if she's sure they're ours,
she says they've eaten all her flowers.

I tuck my PJ's in my wellies
and turn the sound down on the tele'.
I tell her that I'm on my way,
there isn't more that I can say.

I race off with my torch in hand,
this isn't really what I'd planned.
I met the heifers in the lane,
just as I felt it start to rain.

My hair was plastered on my face,
the rounding up became a race.
The neighbour helped and blocked a gap,
it took two hours to get them back.

My PJ's were now flecked with muck,
but that was not the worst of luck.
When I got home I had no keys,
this farming life is not a breeze.

I went next door, they'd gone to bed,
so I walked back down the road instead.
I met my house mate back from the town,
she looked me up, she looked me down.

She saw the hair stuck to my face,
cow muck dried firm on bits of lace.
She laughed and laughed until she cried,
then said let's get you back inside.

She said that I was rather smelly,
Radox mixed with eau de welly.
She said that's not how I'd find love
and then a shout came from above.

It was the guy who lived next door,
we'd always had some sweet rapport.
He said that he would be right down,
I felt a smile replace my frown.

He saw the muck and gave a shrug,
then wrapped me in a loving hug.
He asked me round for a hot drink,
he didn't care about the stink.

And that was thirty years ago,
the memory gives me a glow.
We fell in love that very night,
even though I looked a fright.

We've had our share of ups and downs,
but lots more smiles than we've had frowns.
Our bond is strong, our hearts are true,
and we always say that "I love you".

The Silly Season.

The silly season has begun,
no more nights out, no more fun.
The weather's set on fair and dry,
The sun is shining in the sky.

The grain store waits to hold the yield,
from trailers full from golden fields.
The moisture's checked and all is ripe,
there'll be no early bed tonight.

The combine roars, the header turns.
The joints are greased, the auger churns.
And off they go, the dust flies high
the harvest home starts in July.

Rape Seeds.

Oh the combine wheels are turning
and on every sock and toe,
are tiny little rape seeds
looking for a place to go.

I find them in the bathroom
drifts by the skirting boards,
it is the time to find them
a little rape seed hoard.

They are scattered in the shower
and right around the loo,
it isn't hard to see them
there are more than just a few.

But don't worry it won't last long
if you like to keep things neat,
they'll be finished by next Thursday
and then they start the wheat!

Time For You.

Don't forget to find some time for you once in a while.

None of my friends have ever been
out in the town and not been clean.
They don't have straw stuck in their hair
or wondered why folk stop and stare.

They haven't rushed to get some bread
on the way back from the cow shed,
smelling of cows and udder dip
with specks of muck on brow and lip.

Or ripped their jeans and didn't care
their knickers were exposed to air.
Or had a pocket full of string
and orange elastrator rings.

Women who work upon the land
have forearms that are always tanned.
With wind burnt cheeks and messy hair
because their cows don't really care.

They usually have a blackened nail
that got crushed between a wall and bale.
And purple stains from spraying feet.
With oil and grease the looks complete.

Their cars are full of bits of feed
and stuff the vets says they might need,
the sacks of chaff and odd syringes,
a sledgehammer and packs of hinges.

And in the lounge under a lamp,
a sickly lamb has set up camp.
It staggers up and weakly bleats
next to the basket full of sheets.

And in the fridge some vaccine waits
between the cheese and bag of grapes.
The table groans with bills and bags
and parcels full of new ear tags.

But deep inside there lurks a spark
that wants to scrub up after dark.
Farm girls are stunning and unique
when they wash the muck from off their cheek.

Once in a while they all should go
to see a movie or a show.
Put on high heels and dress up smart,
go out with mates and have a laugh.

They all are special, strong and tough,
but sometimes this is not enough.
It's nice to be spoilt once in a while
and have those nails cleaned with a file.

So don't forget you all deserve
to have your sanity preserved.
Make sure you find some time for you,
between the cows and pigs and ewes.

Arable.

Let's not forget the arable guys and girls!

All may be safely gathered in
and tucked up in the drier.
Thanks have been sung in every church
by every local choir.

For those who work in arable,
it really has just started.
The time to get in next year's crop
is not for the faint-hearted.

They plough a field and then it rains,
they wait for it to dry.
Then work like hell to get it done
with one eye on the sky.

And back and forth they check the soil
and hope that it will go.
If they don't start the drilling,
well only weeds will grow.

The autumn days are getting short,
the leaves fall off the trees.
The forecast talks of showery bursts
to frustrate and to tease.

But then they say that it's set fair
for just about a week.
The grease guns fly, the diesels in,
the drill has had a tweak.

And then it's cakes and sandwiches
to fuel the tractor drivers.
They come out even if they're ill,
you'd never call them skivers.

Up and down they plough the fields
relentless is their task,
balancing a whole pork pie
and coffee in a flask.

They carry on long after dark,
you'll spot them by their lights.
They work the fields all through the day
and long into the night.

Then they come home to get the food
left in the microwave.
They rinse their grime off in the shower,
and the men don't have a shave.

And this goes on week after week
until it's put to bed.
The work that goes on while we sleep
to make sure we're all fed.

Vows.

And what a wedding that would be!

It's three o'clock in the morning,
and the vicar's on the phone.
He says there's a cow in his garden
and he doesn't think it's alone.

I stumble into the bed post
and grab the nearest top.
My leg is stuck in my knickers
and I'm doing a frantic hop.

I scream to my sleeping husband
who hasn't heard a thing;
"The cows are down at the rectory,
didn't you hear the phone ring?"

I'm trying to decide if I have time
to nip to the loo for a wee,
but every second counts when
the cows are out on a spree.

The lights are on in the kitchen,
wellies are pulled on bare feet.
A woolly hat holds my hair down
and the image is complete.

We jump in the old farm landy'
our teeth are all a chatter.
The frost shines bright in the headlights
and we bounce down the drive with a clatter.

Our brains are trying to wake up,
it feels like they're stuffed full of wool,
but when we round the next corner
we come face to face with the bull.

He lifts up his head and bellows,
we see eyes shining bright in the lights.
And right up behind is the vicar
looking like he's had a bad fright.

It seems that the bull had decided
that the heifers were hard to resist.
He'd broken the fence and jumped over
and they'd followed him into the mist.

Along comes the cowman and fiancée,
in pyjamas, wellies and jackets.
Wielding small lengths of plastic
and making a hell of a racket.

The vicar does his best to be helpful
and tries to make them turn back,
but the heifers have got their tails up
and disappear up a track.

Five o'clock in the morning,
it's too late to go back to bed.
So we all roll up in the kitchen
and cook up a breakfast instead.

Next month when the cowman got married,
when they were exchanging their vows,
the vicar asked if they'd promise,
to always fence in their cows!

The Phone Call.

Don't get too hung up cleaning if you have visitors,
they will always find the corner that hasn't been done!

The house has got so filthy that
the dog has moved outdoors.
There's cow muck on the carpet
and oil stains on the floor.

The sink is full of dishes
the washing is piled up,
you can try to make a coffee
but you might not find a cup.

The wellies are invading
and have taken over the porch,
amongst the heaps of overalls
a chainsaw and a torch.

The straw bits are advancing
and have made a little path,
all throughout the kitchen
and in a line around the bath.

There's wormer in the hallway,
it's been there since last May,
because we got distracted
and started making hay.

Some needles and syringes
are nestling in a pan,
in between the cereals
the butter and some jam.

But then we get a phone call
from relations from the city,
they want to come on over
and look at me with pity.

So out come piles of bin bags,
the vacuum and the bleach,
and I hide away the clutter
in cupboards out of reach.

I'm working like a whirlwind,
I'm left to my devices,
I even clean the cooker
and the cupboard full of spices.

But I've left the back door open
and the hens have walked right in.
They have scratched out all the peelings
I had left right by the bin.

And soon I am all polished,
there's a Bloo inside the loo,
the windows have been sparkled
to give them a better view.

I have plugged in lots of AirWicks
and sprayed curtains with Febreze,
and now we smell of cow muck
with a "hint of summer's breeze".

I think I have been clever
and I welcome them inside,
and they sit down on the sofa
and I'm full of inward pride.

But they move a random cushion
and find the head of a dead mouse,
that the cat thought was a present
and had brought into the house.

I can still hear distant screaming
as they run back to their car,
we may not be quite perfect
but I like it just the way we are!

Christmas For Livestock Farmers.

It's Christmas Day in the morning
and it's peeing down with rain.
The cows are in for milking,
so here we go again.

As all the country wakes up
in central heated bliss,
I am in the parlour,
covered in muck and piss.

So when you make your cuppa,
a steaming mug of tea.
When you put the milk in,
spare a thought for me.

And every livestock farmer
will be out there getting wet.
Filling troughs and feeders
hoping they don't need a vet.

They'll all go in for breakfast
when all is checked and fed,
calves have milk in their bellies,
there's fresh straw in every shed.

Thanks to all of the farmers
especially on Christmas Day,
setting out hay and silage
in an all they can eat buffet.

But you will be rewarded
you're bound to get new socks.
A penknife and a hoodie,
aftershave in a posh box.

And when you've eaten dinner
and the kids want to play games,
you'll be sat by the fireplace snoring
(I know 'cause you're all the same)!

The Storm.

This was written after watching the terrible storms in America and seeing on the news the utter devastation.

The world watches with bated breath,
the storm drives on as dark as death.
Some are already lost or drowned,
as others flee to safer ground.

Relentless as the hounds of hell
it flattens towns to just a shell.
We see the agonising plight
and weep at the devastating sight.

The farmers mark their stock in hope.
Releasing gates, undoing rope.
They pray that nature helps them through,
there's nothing else that they can do.

The roads are blocked, the gas runs dry,
the children are too shocked to cry.
They've done their best to be prepared,
but everyone is running scared.

The wind picks up the falling leaves,
and cruelly whistles through the trees.
The ones who made the choice to stay,
can only sit and wait and pray.

The fearsome force of nature's wrath,
destroys whatever is in it's path.
There is no more that they can do,
they have to trust that they'll get through.

And in the darkness of the night,
we all must send a guiding light,
and help with whatever we can spare,
and hope someone listens to their prayer.

On Loan.

Their legacy is still with us if you have the vision to see.

I gaze across the land and glimpse
the farmers of yesteryear.
In the gentle dip of the valley so green,
The stream still so crystal clear.

Their memories live in every hedge,
in every tree, flower and copse.
The distant horizon shrouded in mist
where the worry and heartache stops.

The gnarled ancient oak, centuries old
that marks the edge of the wood.
Where the broken stile leads over the hill
to where the cow shed stood.

Their whispers still blow on the breeze
telling of hardship and pain.
The dusty days gazing up to the skies
looking for clouds full of rain.

The ancient rolls of well worked land
hold the secrets of horses and plough.
A rusted out hay rake forgotten and lost
grown over by sycamore boughs.

The path to the ford worn down through the years
by sheep on their way to the dip.
The whistles still hang on the fresh summer breeze,
"Here, Rosie, here, Bouncer and Gip".

The boundaries marked by age old stone walls
built for our future with care.
The views to the hills that still draw the eye
where time lets you stand still and stare.

The land is eternal, it's only on loan
it's your turn to pick up the reins.
Until your sun sets, you return to the earth
whilst the hill and the valley remains.

Your Sweet Smiling Face.

The sun is still shining so bright,
as we hug our children so tight.
The buttercups bloom
just the same as last year.
The rivers still flow
with water so clear.
The birds are still singing
the songs of the air.
The bees are still feeding
on sweet free nectar.
Life keeps on going,
the beat of our hearts.
The buzz of the traffic,
the noise of the cars.
The shops are all open,
a man collects trolleys.
And children queue up
to buy ice cream and lollies.
Schools are crammed full
with students in chairs,
And bankers research
the stocks and the shares.
The clock keeps on ticking,
the world goes on turning.
The rivers are flowing,
fires keep on burning.
The earth doesn't know

of the hatred of man,
as families hold on
the best as they can.
The mountains, the canyons
the valleys and plains.
The heat of the sun
and the power of the rain.
The stars in the sky
remain up in space,
as we try to make sense
why we're here in this place.
And we watch and we wonder
and ask ourselves why,
someone can decide
when it's our turn to die.
And the years will fly past,
the winters and spring.
In time we will learn
to deal with death's sting.
But the memories of love
will stay in our hearts.
And the evil will wither
and the sadness depart.
The earth will roll on,
It's old journey through space,
but we'll never forget
your sweet smiling face.

Time Out.

The day is done you've had a shower,
you're smelling now more like a flower.
Cow muck is scrubbed from fingernails,
all part of what the job entails.

The dog is curled up on his bed,
he's happy that he's warm and fed.
The kettle's on, the cottage pie
is smelling good I cannot lie.

The lights burn bright, the fire is lit,
it's time to settle down a bit.
The socks come off with bits of straw,
the wellies wait by the back door.

It's time to rest that weary back,
and cut yourself a little slack.
And grab yourself a cup of tea
and have a look what's on TV.

Then chat about the farming day,
and have your dinner on a tray.
This is what life is all about,
the precious time when you chill out.

You know you've done your very best
and now it's time to have a rest.
You check to see if it will rain,
or will you get to haul the grain.

And then your eyes will start to close,
you settle down for a small doze.
Content to know your stock are fed
and you can sleep content in bed.